Red Letter Days

Books by Mekeel McBride

No Ordinary World
The Going Under of the Evening Land
Red Letter Days

Limited Edition

A Change in Weather

Red Letter Days

poems by
Mekeel McBride

Carnegie Mellon University Press
Pittsburgh 1988

Acknowledgments

Grateful acknowledgement is made to the following publications in which these poems first appeared:

Boston Review: "Transmigration"
Cyphers: "Suitcase, Unaccompanied"
The New Yorker: "Growing Stones in New Hampshire"
Nimrod: "The Short Autobiography of Inspiration"
The Ontario Review: "After Grief"
                     "If I'd Been Born in Tennessee"
                     "Red Letters"
Pequod: "Solstice"
Ploughshares: "Annunciation"
               "Matins"
               "The Mechanics of Repair"
               "Taking Pleasure"
Poetry: "The Earliest Maps"
          "Castaway"
          "My Story as Told by Someone Else"
Seneca Review: "The Relative Distance of the Stars"
Southwest Review: "River"
Tendril: "The Kiss"
          "Lessons"
          "The Thief of Light"
Three Rivers Poetry Journal: "Onion"
                              "The Influence"

With thanks to Gary Bromley, Jay Apt, Mimi White, Barbara Cairns, Roland LaBrie, David Campbell and Jane Shore.

The publication of this book is supported by grants from the National Endowment for the Arts in Washington, D.C., a Federal agency, and by the Pennsylvania Council on the Arts.

Contents

IV

For Kathleen Romaine McBride

And so the world changes daily
under our feet and the dolphins
themselves rise up in our sleep
reciting the Lord's Prayer . . .

Dale Kushner

Red Letters

Hot-spit-and-damn of unchartable cargo flashes past
lightning blessed. Bridge shakes, almost shatters
with the passing. Gone, and then it's gone. Train

rumbling and plummeting out of summer air. Honest
in its passage, shakes bones, blooms hair. Seduces
and then stands you up, hopeless in one long whistle blast,

almost gets you there, getting and getting. Lackawanna
cars swollen with omniscient thunder, coffins, cheap
wine from Hungary. Gives you soot-stained wind,

a lust for the long worthless wheatfields of America.
Makes sealed baggage cars sing out their locked contents:
gladiola, apple, Aunt-So-and-So's black lace-up shoes,

a last letter from death row, nothing but snow
sealed under the silk skins of Maine potatoes. Shamelessly
invades the bedrooms of the unhappily married, inventing

their semi-tropical dreams of parole. Prudence, absent
even in the once-was-blue caboose. Won't be back
with its bereaved sheep grazing in the tiny meadow

of a boxcar next to the red letters of separated lovers.
Keeps no schedule, keeps nothing, and keeps going,
mad sweetheart to each steadfast tree it passes,

spits its way into the future, dragging with it
tracks and vantage point, sunset and perspective,
marries them all in a black daze of closed horizon

leaving only a slight sigh in the shaken trees, no birth
of storm, just ordinary dusk and the common burden
of having to admit that being witness was enough.

I

The Earliest Maps

In the earliest maps, the ocean
advances in carefully inked-in
margins: *As far as we have gone*. Then,
What we could see from there. It's here
the world ends abruptly in a roar of celestial
water that pours far past imagination.

But look at the part marked *Where we
are*, inhabited fat as an ant hill.
The mapmaker has drawn in women and men
bending to garden and anvil, scarcely
aware there is an edge to anything.
And tangled in their hair so haphazardly

you might not notice, sea-serpents bloom
while fish with stubby wings half-glide,
half-flail in the brain's blue
mutiny, a tea cup of it but enough
to support even the whale, robed
in brocades of barnacle, shipwreck and star.

Now scan to the map's real ocean far past
Where we have been. There, ungainly beasts
entice the eye as they breed and feast, huge
in size but strange in thought for that
has been painted in, the windows
of their cranial huts thrown open. Look—

bright tapestries of benevolent dreaming—
tiny women push wheelbarrows full
of turnips; a turf-cutter's hearth glows
gold as a grain of sand. And all of earth's
rivers, no more than blue currants, crushed
sweet in the beast's outstretched hand.

After Grief

Oyster shell and mussel shell
float on each wave's edge
like the small boats
moonlight might use
for full scale invasion.
But this is sunrise, tide out;
blue pools glow with whole stones
and a frail anemone opens
like an invalid's heart
toward a slow appraisal
of light. Let the man
who walks here be without
fishing pole or oyster pail,
wading boots or net.
If a day moon floats
over his shoulder full
of autumn and salt, that is just
as well. Let his own body,
cool and salty itself
be nothing more than happy
student in the wind's
blue school.

The Kiss

In an empty room two people kiss
and it becomes a university.
As first Dean, the Kiss wallpapers
each classroom with redwood forests,
star charts from the childhood
of Nostradamus. Clear tranquility of rain
invited in to give guest lectures.
And angels, their wings swelling
like orchids, like peach orchards
teach wool-gathering, loitering.

Valentines arrive from the ghosts
of forgotten children, invisible
twins long neglected. And textbook
representatives leave free seed catalogs,
samples of rare August-blooming lilies.
Papers appear about the Kiss, first
praise, then the careful critical approach.
Finally, claims of larceny, infidelity,
perjury. Meetings occur in rooms
with impeccable roofs,
the interiors as dark as the heart
of a politician. Secret votes taken.

Found lacking. Eased out. The Kiss,
that shy zodiac spinning
in glitter-filled laughter
through inestimable dark,
doesn't have the sense to worry.
Instead, studies in solitude
the common sense scripture of seagull wings
sweeping winter's iciest sky.
Then investigates meadow mice,
poultice roots, and the sacred
potato—all inheritors
of the misunderstood underground.

Invents the healing property of one
snowflake caught and cherished
in the black hair of the crippled girl.
Oh, and it built a house, the Kiss did,
a very small house in the shining disk
of a thrown penny, descending
into the bottomless well of a possible wish.
And it lives there, reading
the love letters Marco Polo wrote
to continents he never discovered.
In the end, insisting on nothing but this—
in an empty room, that two people kiss.

The Relative Distance of the Stars

No news is good
news a friend says,
his father's heart
ticking, stopping—
no music in
the metronome
expensive home
for the dying.
I'm agreeing
writing to you:
saw one gold leaf
maple drift loose
confetti light
sway down cradle–
slow then catch hold
against the grain
brown trunk of its
own tree, solace,
map, and source of
sunrise displayed
in veins small gold
poster, wanted
most wanted I
tell you it was
like finding at
the shoulder blade
one fire-light wing
beginning to
unfold.

for David Campbell

Transmigration

The lingering scripture of bleach
praised itself in each towel and sheet
while insect-starred roses
stitched the red thread of sweet
July into the collars and stiff cuffs
of our well-worn summer clothes.

Coarse rope, tied from elm to elm,
like the line of white a child
will sometimes draw for heaven,
held us all bodiless and pure
in that distant air. My mother's pastel dresses,
inhabited by wind, swayed, almost danced
as she danced in the kitchen alone

and the sleeves of my father's weekday shirts
pointed to a day moon, tree stump,
the white wheelbarrow,
as if looking were lesson enough or cure
for the slight ache at the shoulder
where the colorless V of clothespin

kept with soldierly pinches
the float and swell of drying clothes
in place. And so a day might pass, give way
to the setting sun through a backyard tree,
making a foreign lace, a frail brocade
of nightgowns, blouses, handkerchieves

and wind invaded them with such levity
that I could guess at their escape;
ghost clothes blue in the evening air
like odd birds or aliens migrating slowly
over houses, trees, a whole tribe
of cloud-grazing nomads. Then one blouse

drops, the white one my mother wore on holidays,
the one with rhinestones at the collar
and the sleeves; each replica gem
silly with star glitter, the gossip of comets.
All of this to be claimed, taken in, submitted
to the hissing oracle of the small flat iron,

then blessed away into the dark kingdoms
of wardrobe and drawer—
like souls who believe nothing
can be lost, nothing dies—waiting
in windless dark, in summer sleep
to be taken out again and worn.

for my mother

Available Light

I'll tell you
who I write for—the houseplants—
outside all summer;
now, first frost, cloistered
in calm, indoor weather, especially
the geranium.

As leggy as any chorus line dancer
it kicks up and up
for whatever difference
one inch makes
in its proximity
to sun.

All that stretching and then
half its leaves
grow gold, drop, as I stoke
the woodstove, layer
myself in sweaters the color
of fire.
I've been told
repeatedly

by nursery people
geraniums won't keep over winter
unless you hang them
upside down in newspaper hoods
in a dark cellar.
As a child,

for punishment, I was made
to stand for hours
in a black stairwell corner
to consider my ill temper
but I knew those walls
were honeycombed
with treasure—

bracelets of Egyptian gold,
red-handled jump ropes, turtles
who could swallow whole lakes
and I used my time
standing in the dark
figuring ways to rescue

what was rightfully
mine. October, I place
the geranium
in the brightest window
I can find
where it shapes itself
to available light
and stays alive.

The Proper Offering

"I should have been a gardener, he
told himself, or a woodsman. Maybe
a policeman. But a shepherd would
have been best of all. . . .
He suspected he no longer
daydreamed."
                —Mark Smith
                The Delphinium Girl

1. The Gardener

Blank clock of the sunflower
towers over us, leans a little toward earth
as birds tick away at the ripe seeds.
Ask only for what you need, my father said,
but every year new wildflowers
bless the unused meadow
as if my joy had taken root
with a peculiar lack of boundary.
It is simple enough. My son
pinches the last day lily, nibbles
one by one, the bronze petals,
sneezes, now wears
a moustache of golden pollen.

2. The Woodsman

Maybe in the unused palace
of forest—an axe, a new persistence
to get through, clear the air
then shuffle rough lumber
into a hut with no lamp, star, unsettling
map of light to this dark ballroom
where love letters
from wren and grackle slip through
cracked glass; and rain spits in, too,
like some cantankerous old fool
finishing up a story he's told

only to himself and
to himself, laughs,
anyway.

3. The Policeman

On horseback. No assault
from sirens, no ice-light
targeting the more than likely innocent,
no locked channel chatter
from the black CB. Just this big chestnut,
the obedient clop of horse-shoe to cement,
an occasional stop for him to nip
city zinnias from a window box.
Nights, my pockets blossoming with apples,
I steal him from the stable and we gallop
until the stars, from their ordered places,
swing loose in a river of silver and sugar
and we slip past.

4. The Shepherd

About the sheep, there is not much
that can be said: meadow-grazers,
tame mowers; and the grass, too,
simply repeats. Here, I don't need much sleep.
The cradle of a cloud offers itself
but I stay where I am, drowsy
in the sound of goat bells spilling
over it all. Here, alpine blue's no color
other than a flower and a rough
and musty cheese reinvents
the golden wheel.
I write this. Someone will read:
As it should be. Evening. Healed.

II

Growing Stones in New Hampshire

That first year we turned the soil,
charted a garden that even Babylon
might have blessed. But we had not
guessed about the stones,
what a heavy work they would make
for us—something neither of us had foreseen.

Making way for one radish might mean
shovelling up stones the size
of sewing baskets; for cabbage,
dislodging rock that weighed more
than our woodstove; and in exchange
for tomatoes, a boulder bigger than a sofa.

But we got the garden in
and even had a harvest
after slugs and woodchuck, cutworm
and drought. "Next year," we said,
"will be better. We'll build a fence.
At least the stones are out."

In May, when we set spade to soil
there they were again but worse,
as if they had, in the middle of winter,
descended, winnowed back through solid earth
to where we'd first disturbed their sleep,
returned with even their most distant relatives.

One shovel broke and then another.
Seedlings we'd begun indoors failed
for no apparent reason. "Never mind,"
you said, "we'll harvest what we have."
Evenings you inspect that odd, half-turned over
plot. "Looks like a good crop,"

you say, "and easy. No wasted water.
No weeding to be done."

And start to think those stones are yours,
a yield, a kind of sign. "Sculpture,"
you insist, and talk of trailing them all the way
to Boston or New York.

Lessons

1.
Denied: the secret notebook of roots
hidden beneath every step I take,
where earthworms curl
like apostrophes
at the feet of stones,
where the snake dreams, the hedgehog laments
nothing.

These things, even these,
have been denied.

2.
The sky remains empty
like the back room in a museum
closed off by blue velvet ropes.
There are no trees,
only the bent arm of a cactus
scribbled by a sad child
who should have been doing her lessons.

Emptiness opens its little cafe
and does a lively business.

3.
You can't possibly know.
Even drought's bouquet of dead grass remembers
Eden and accepts that loneliness
for what it's worth. My eyes open
to everything
and I can't even locate
the little peasant girl

who wears shoes of daylight and goes
where she needs to, where she wants.

4.
Here, behind the blue cafe, I wait.
The deaf old man reshingling the roof
would somehow know and like me less
if I began to sing.
You can't possibly understand.
The words were diamonds. The words
were amulets the moon dreamed up
on its day off.

Now the curator, in colorless gloves,
pins them to an impersonal heaven of black burlap.

5.
You are sitting in a room
somewhere. It is evening. It is a country
untroubled by earthquakes. Darkness
returns quietly from the wedding
with no keepsake. Evening
and still you have failed to notice
the cocoon, the loom, the black scissors.
And yes, it has already started,

although you do not notice,
the June-bug's dark and ceaseless prayer.

Castaway

The island, gone,
with only one telephone call for help
safe in the pure air of the rescuer's ear.
But do not hope
that those about to arrive

will understand. Do not wonder
that they cannot find us
in our green canoe of forgotten orchards,
in this small ache of a boat.
They do the best they can.

Iceburg! they cry repeatedly
into a sorcerer's wind. Perhaps if there were less
fog, they might see. Perhaps.
But I have time only to instruct myself
in ancient matters. Better

to carve stars in the palm
of my hand than to attempt
making sense of this immense loneliness. I know.
I was one of the first to drown
and it is an unpleasant thing to breathe water

so intimate with those who have no knowledge
of the weightlessness of other atmospheres.
It is fair, then, to try to believe
in something. That we are not dead.
That the white cottage has already reinvented

itself. You might, for instance,
be moving with precise joy
to join a woman in that simple kitchen.
There, little moons of freshly sliced garlic
glitter on the chopping block;

in a glowing bowl old world bread rises,
sweet with almonds and caraway seed.
No need to weep, my friend, with so much water
all around us. The soup has been salted enough.
It is just a story, just a story I tell,
my little jest against nothingness.

The Influence

Tiny as a cocktail-time toothpick,
she grazes her way
through the houseplants on the windowsill
then, for show, swings from a spider plant vine,
falls into a fica, nibbles leaves
that would kill a housepet
but she survives. Concocts
a megaphone from an old grocery list
to let me know all about her weather.

Otherwise, how could I hear her
over boiling coffee water,
telephone's black warble,
the insatiable vacuum? She cries, "I've given up
everything to live with you."
This is true. She used to have a house,
real children, a car red as forest fire.
But then she was befriended
by a knife-thrower from a wintering circus.

Night after night, he polished the hard
silver edges while admitting
his past history: ex-opera star,
ruined voice, renegade daughter. She, silent,
shrank to the size
of a clothespin's dance partner
then appeared one morning
under my pillow, white
and angry as a child's lost tooth.

Now she bites holes in my best sweaters,
almost drowns trying to drink
perfume, mostly uses the megaphone
for lectures on the weakening
of my moral fiber.
When guests come over
she makes herself smaller,

slips aboard the replica ship
trapped mastless in an old wine bottle.

She sweeps across the matchstick deck
banking, as usual, on better winds,
good crew, tides that do
as they're told. Owns the ocean the way
a politician pockets but never weeps
into a fine silk handkerchief.
And on the splinter of that dark departure plank
falls, small heap of bird bones,
into another numb sleep.

Annunciation

Scarecrow, they called me, in my old gingham, poked
up on a pole to tilt
and waltz with whatever fickle wind happened by.
My blood, bone and heart: old stable straw
ticking with crickets, locusts, every
harvest hungry insect.

For years I watched this garden someone else planted.
Limbs all akimbo, pure
as a saint, I danced. Pauper of weather,
mother of fear, my smallest gesture
scattered grackle, crow, rabbit, vole.

Nights, the tiny votive lights of a galaxy
faltered, went out; match-scratch,
shooting star. It never mattered. I was not able
to make a wish. The farmer and his wife paid me
no mind. So I, creature neither of heaven
nor of earth taught every other animal exile.

Who knows what made the small crow light on my shoulder
as awake as a meteor. Only one note
shuddering from his open throat: escape.
An annunciation, all right, but for angel
carrion eater, and for ears, my hearing all too tuned
to the scritch of mice, the heavy thud
of the farmer's shovel.

Matins

In the little casket, a garden begins to grow:
wild roses pink as the mouths of house cats,
daisies going to pieces
in a *loves me, loves me not* lullaby,
the white light of calla lilies
flooding the vault's wall.
Is there a baby in the casket? Yes,
the blue kingdom inhabited by you, my twin,
skin stained by birth's red mark, lying quietly
among the oddly consensual flowers.

A father, suspended like the Hanged Man
in the Tarot deck floats over, upside down
his wild electric hair, a blue benediction
over your troubled sleep. He sings
forgiveness, the names of birds and herbs
in death's golden country.
The clock, a cricket in a bamboo cage
to accompany on the fusty violin
of body scraping against itself
this autumn, this song almost gone.

In the little casket, a kerosene lamp
blond tulip, foolishly recites on one
glowing abacus bead all of its accomplishments.
Here, it sputters, flower or flame,
untamed accountant of the heart's vast debt.
Night would like to devour this
but the music swells, the cocoon splits open
and a stained glass angel
unfurls one wing behind the curtain
of tear-rise and eye-blink.

From among the ranks of the crow-robed mourners
someone whispers, "I saw
the body move." In the little casket, a grandmother
carries the infant through a greenhouse

where wild morning glories flourish,
stops at the replica of an English garden,
a sturdy dazzle of hot house air.
Beyond, where only an oblique glance
can find true passage: a simple house,

one oil lamp, cricket at the black stone hearth,
and in the eastern most room—dawn,
a white camellia, a cradle song.
If you could get to it, the Lazarus tomb.

for Ivan Lalić

The Point of Highest Stress

They are almost born, the astronauts,
curled bud-like into the capsule

hurling toward the beautiful blank
that begets most notions of heaven.

The shuttle leaves earth easily;
white smoke of lift-off

banners out like headlines
the papers never print;

Peace Negotiations A Success.
One minute, twelve seconds into launch

the Captain says, "Go with throttle up"
and the shuttle's in Max Q, the point

of highest stress. Sudden nova
of the explosion

forms in holiday fireworks
scorpion, crab or dragon.

When the smoke expands
into an extravagant chrysanthemum—

light blooming into light—the mind,
before it can translate, insists

the shuttle continues, safe, surely
safe, though out of sight. Slowly

the television camera swings back
to the crowd—standing still

as the lava-stiff deceased
of Pompeii. Later, grief and myth marry

in a eulogy promising the astronauts, lost
in one blind eye-blink of human error,

are now, somehow, kin to the stars
they longed to travel through.

But they knew where they were going;
their risks: honest,

pumped in and out like oxygen,
their face masks clean and clear.

Now, they're where they are.
It's the bystanders whose faces

the camera focuses, separate, in disbelief.
Though all parts belong to the whole,

those left on the ground forget that of hope,
praise, and bone, only bone gives way—

in one heartbeat—the rest heals.
This law holds.

The Mechanics of Repair

How did I spend my evening?
By coming home in rain that slowly
translated itself into curtain after curtain
of oriental beads that I brushed through
cold and very tired.
All winter the repairman
has come dressed in sweaters,
never coats, crouched in darkness
at the heart of things, trying to perform
the mechanics or repair.

The first time, he had to chip open
the furnace door, cemented
by past tenants, saying *You can't*
tell a thing unless you can see the flame.
I brought him coffee, whiskey that last time
he knelt on the icy floor at one a.m.
and still the furnace wouldn't start.
Tonight, I don't even call. Finally, it's clear
when a thing's past fixing.

As last antidote to this endless chill
I make myself invent Maikiska, a Yugoslavian
in her thirties, old world flowers
braided in her long brown hair.
She will speak no ill of me nor hear
ill spoken. Her English, sweet as almonds,
needs no real correction. In her own country
she would be a duchess, if regimes
could be erased. *If, if,* she suddenly says,

and her laughter is a church full
of votives lighting all at once.
If is word you use like city people
light fireplace for party. Throw in kerosene.
Big flame but no fire after that.
For you we need kindling and paper, kindling

and little match. About emptiness
she has nothing to say. So I cook
black mushrooms, gingered pork,
chinese noodles clear as glass.

Then take a shower, relieved to stand
under something in my control.
Outside, a matter of degree and rain
translates itself into another thing
entirely. A neighbor, penitent and tender,
leans over, with a flashlight and old sheets,
his snow-dusted crocuses, unaware
they can, alone, survive this weather.
How odd, after all, to find myself
speaking brokenly, aloud, claiming

birth in a foreign country, all for the sake
of possessing again the delicate mechanism
of flame. I settle under the quilt
that took me seven years to sew; my sheets,
a very simple blue, no real way
to say how blue they are: child's pinafore,
morning sky pure in a forgiving mirror.
Sleep, embrace, something essential endures.
Lullaby, whispers Maikiska, *listen.*

The Angel

Glass bottle filling with the pink
milk of sunrise. Foreign man

on a unicycle spilling away the whole
icy hill

under one silver wheel. Archipelago
of a cat asleep on the carpet:

start of a civilization sparked
by one paw-twitch. The appearance

of the angel
sears off outer garments

of the petty crook, organ grinder,
true potentate and gourmet cook.

Exposed: the awkwardness
of our shoelaces-untied trip

into the neighbor's compost heap.
Small islands of orange rind

over which rises the rough star
of crushed egg shell—what was waste

will be enough. For angelic assistance,
don't look up.

III
The Short Autobiography of Inspiration

1. Inspiration's Anatomy

Begins with the ordinary wishbone of a common chicken hung with sewing thread in the kitchen to dry. For days or weeks it develops the invisible flesh of wish and desire. Sways, little divining rod, over the woman washing dishes, chopping onions, rinsing garden earth from her hands. When it is finally dry and ready to be used, it will weigh scarcely more than spilled salt or the petals, drifted loose, from peonies on the kitchen table. Because the woman is alone she must name one wish for her right hand, another for the left, then split the fragile bone to see which of the desires overrides. It is one of the conditions of inspiration that things must come apart before they can be put back together.

2. Inspiration's Tactics

Dinner and breakfast dishes lie undone in the sink. The child wants to be taken to the zoo. Your husband's under the car, humming something the Beach Boys used to sing. The dog needs to be walked. Mostly, you would like to doze in a chair on the sunny lawn, as tranquil as the neighbor's ornamental flamingo. But the dog insists on going now and so you leave, later quite surprised to see you've gone further than you usually do. In this strange part of town you meet an old man. Eighty three, he says, standing on his immaculate lawn. Maybe he's lonely, maybe only sensible, but he invites you to sit under the kingdom of a huge ginko tree. He tells you a sea captain brought it ninety years ago from Africa, the only female ginko in the area. He knows local history, old stories, relates the one about short Henry who fell in love with Cordelia. She was very tall. Some sort of fight occured and then Cordelia died, unmarried. Henry buried her dog beside her and on the grave placed the statue of a weeping bride. When Henry passed away, he was placed next to Cordelia with his dog as well. The old man gives you directions to the graveyard and you have no difficulty locating the weeping bride. She is quite lovely but you wonder who would chisel such grief into permanence. Her garland of stone flowers has fallen out of her hand, forever out of her own stone gaze. You are relieved to see how much she does not resemble you. In case ghosts exist you stay and speak with them, the lovers who may only sleep together under earth, and their patient animals. But it is the stone bride who makes you return again and again with fresh flowers that you place directly in her line of vision. If there is one thing inspiration loves above all, it is the stories, the odd details of other people's lives. For this reason, inspiration is the original shape-changer and in this case, conspired to get you out of the house by fetching its leash and dancing in front of the open door.

3. Inspiration's Laboratory

In the laboratory of the dream, all experiments are executed and recorded, made available to you by morning. Inspiration always leaves a clue, a gift, a remnant on the front porch of your waking. As common as the newspaper, so common you often overlook it, small as a key or coin, clear as a window, the word or image that wasn't important before. Here in the dream, inspiration hides its private journals, its half-finished blueprints. Your childhood is there, not simply recorded, but real in the small glass paperweight where it snows or doesn't, depending on how you hold it. Your future, too, takes shape in odd pastels or the erotic colors of the tropics and although you rarely remember having anything to do with it, frequently you find your hands flecked with drying paint. Understand that it is in the room of the dream that inspiration redeems itself and requires that you do the same.

4. What Inspiration Does In Its Spare Time

Quilting or car repair, anything that requires careful attention to detail; supplies, as end result, the useful. The insistent order of the crossword puzzle where words breed and dream in each other, where *inspiration* itself may be the vertical, the sail for horizontal *levity*. Of course the idea of the useful seems to dwindle when one thinks of birdwatching, blessedly nameless birds beginning their raucous cantatas exactly at the moment light begins. Or parachuting, where practice absolves the fear of high power lines and broken legs as one falls more and more in love with the flawed topography of this earth. For inspiration, the useful and the useless are of equal importance.

5. Inspiration's Preoccupation with Reflection

It goes gladly to any mirror, from purse compact to ballroom extravaganza but above all would always choose a lake. There it is at home with the clear surface, happy to share it with the passing shadow of a snowy egret. And under the water surface, the invisible, is, as usual, busy contracting itself out to miracle that later appears as a small, pebble-shelled turtle. Unlike human beings, inspiration adores itself, loves to see itself taking shape.

6. Inspiration's Relationship To Fear

Summer has just occurred and you walk along a deserted beach that consists of granite chips and rock. As you walk you watch the various geometrics the edges make, as well as the indecipherable hieroglyphs of wind on calm water. But you are alone, vulnerable to any stranger. That's fear for you, arriving at the worst possible moment and taking over with complete authority. You start back to the car and halfway there, pick up a stone that's only a little bigger than your hand. On one side you notice a white circle, as if after decades, the full moon passing over has left its perfect print. You could, if you had to, use this as a weapon. But you don't have to and so you stay for the rest of the day. Inspiration will tell you that what you need is always right at hand. Necessity comes into play, I suppose, as the mother of invention, but let's be honest. Invention never was a single child. Its Siamese twin, inspiration, was the one born with the single large heart they both share.

7. When You Think Inspiration Is Gone

This large pink shell might never again be near the sea, never again be home to the perpetually wandering hermit crab. Now it appears to be pure ornament on a coffee table. However, it has taken in air all the way to the back of its smallest spiral chamber. This is one of the places inspiration likes to hide, prides itself on being able to fit into the smallest space, likes the sense that its sleep is often mistaken for the sound of the sea.

8. Inspiration's Meditation on the Difference Between Prose and Poetry

If one is the train speeding through the small dark towns of Ohio headed for the coast, then the other is a red unicycle that carries the blindfolded woman high above the entire circus. Or it's the castle of the copper beech to the star embedded in the morning glory. This could go on and on. If one is X, the other is Z. If you want it made any clearer, poetry lives in the exact center that the two lines of X make, that mysterious crossroad, that constant variable. Prose is forever entertaining itself on the crooked ski-slope of Z where the destination, though often guessed, is never certain. But I can tell you, inspiration has no real interest in this exercise, finds the difference between prose and poetry an arbitrary excuse to be verbose.

9. How Inspiration Deals With The Demands Of The Domestic

Well, it doesn't really care that there are ants walking all over the counters like pilgrims taking over the New England coast. Go ahead and buy ant spray and ant traps but as you prepare for this small-scale war, inspiration has gone wandering off into your past to find you as a child playing dress up. You open your mother's jewelry box. Because there has been recent rain, and because she's left candy inside, the jewelry box has become a small condominium full of red ants that look to you like crazy, animate rubies. You play for hours, opening and closing the lid, monitoring that odd populace as it scurries over pearls and diamond rings. Now, present tense, inspiration returns you to yourself. You seal the sugar in a jar and throw the spray and traps away. Inspiration, in the end, has no understanding of your problems with domestic responsibility. It has one job, one job only, and that is to instigate and propagate delight.

10. Where Inspiration Has Learned A Thing Or Two

From the trees because they are the true intuitives. Palm-readers of sunlight and storm, calm interpreters for any kind of wind, doing most of the detective work on shooting stars and aurora borealis. Their easy-come, easy-go romances with migrating birds scarcely bear recording and not even the quick cinema jump-cuts from summer to snow bother them. Even if there is snow, temperature in the minus numbers, something continues to live, invisible, at the core. Looking at the tree, you might see in the bare branches only the bones of Babayaga's hand or the possibility of kindling for your woodstove, owl-haven, or a kind of living elegy blessed on the highest branch by one thin crow. Of course you would be wrong. What inspiration looks like is never really what it is.

11. Inspiration's Favorite Foods

A freshly baked loaf of black bread where it is rumored that the Brothers Grimm still hide their best stories. Strawberries. Day lilies for salad. And lobster, only if served on a bed of watercress and white violets. In times of stress, the shy solace of a potato. But remember this. Inspiration can, if forced, take nourishment from nothing at all.

12. Why Inspiration Values Air

Let's say grief has insisted you carry its heavy luggage no matter what else you're doing. Let's say you have no choice in the matter. Driving home on an interstate, you see something odd from the corner of your eye and stop the car. It's understood that you have to lug out into the open grief's makeup case, shoe boxes, steamer trunks. But all the while you keep your eye on the bird that stopped you in the first place, bigger than any bird you've ever seen, each sweep of its enormous wings, reminiscent of ancient Egypt, the gorgeous sway of Cleopatra's gray dress as she dances alone slowly in her light-filled chambers. It seems impossible that simple air is what this bird uses for its ascent. You have taken a deep breath and hold it in as if to hold the bird within you; air, the one thing that connects you both. You will learn that you have seen a great blue heron and that they are always grey. Later, just as you are about to fall asleep, you remember that you left every piece of grief's baggage at the side of the road. This, then, is the dream you have:

You walk with an elegant woman into the back yard and see several birds with indigo and emerald breasts. All of them, as large as humans, lift up in flight.

Your friend says, "Not birds. Ballerinas. And you can do what they are doing."

Sure enough, they are long-necked ballerinas, diamonds and lilies in their hair, their blue and green wings like water-color brushes preparing the sky with dusk. You join them in this flight. Only when you look down and see how tiny the earthbound have become do you feel fear.

Then, a chest of drawers appears, miles high and you land on top, terrified. One of the ballerinas flies so near you recognize her as your elegant friend.

She says, "Only your fear makes you immobile. Only your fear stops you from doing what you want to do."

It's not so much that you don't trust yourself. It's just a long way down and you are unaccustomed to wings that work. Still, there is nothing to do but step off the edge. As you glide back to earth you feel that the spirit of the heron has somehow entered you.

The dream, in fact, is a gift from the great blue heron that had its breeding ground in the breath you took and held. You may use it any way you wish, in a painting or a poem, as a story to tell a friend over lunch or as a private reference point. If inspiration is to take in breath, receive a gift, then exhalation is to return the gift after bettering it.

for Joseph Anton

IV

Chair

Chair, you are somewhat like me.
Only quiet. And content to follow, shadow
just after sunrise, as I pull you

away from the table, navigate you,
obedient ship, nearer the open window,
its ocean of cloud. But I do not own you.

Limb crook of an old oak bore you,
brave little wooden nest. It is to all trees
you belong. I am only one woman

heavier than any weather and yet
you endure me. Spoons you understand
and abandoned shoes.

Animals you do not think of often
though your daydream wanders
into the meadow where an old horse

walks awkwardly as a marionette.
Each spindled knob
of your hard back: proof that abacus,

clock-tick, rosary bead
and sentence-end are no more than false
admonishment from the smallest gods.

Solstice

At the turn of the century, we could feel
how war would sweep the continents,
ash and charred bone become the new Bibles.

Our wristwatches were made of glass
so we could see the beautiful, heart-broken gears
spin in strict and separate cosmologies.

And for decades, when the ocean intervened,
like a blue priest, like a solitary scholar,
we said we understood.

You told me how the white horse followed you
out of the city, bony, bloody, its hooves
caked with human excrement.

You could not feed it, would not burden it
even with your thin body. You slept
on brown needles from a dying pine.

At the turn of the century, only the sky
stayed pure, except for a hawk, its hover
only an ancient feint to fool prey.

Black wish. Not even the word goodbye. Once
we met in a white room. I don't remember where.
Fingerprints stained the low ceiling: message

from the invisible prisoner. Outside, mute
nuns walked by counting rosary beads
the color of unripe pears.

After You Died

After you died, you forgot me.
But I found your great black coat pockets
still loud with keys.
So many doors now beg alms.
So many abandoned orchards.
Why is it, then, you cherish
what you do not use?

I cannot help it, I want to hear goat bells,
see you lying in high grass, at peace,
eating ripe cheese, laughing at the error.
But no, you are heard to boast, "Death
is good to me.
Death gives me what I want."

And so you greet the broom as`friend
then, preoccupied, sweep
narrow corridors of the old hotel.
At your waist, keys to the basement
with its floor of earth, keys
to the boarded-up attic. After labor,
you winnow sleep from dark wine.

Only in the garden do I dare speak
these things. Here, lettuce opens,
ancient bible. And beans
faithfully convey into this world
their green prayer beads.
Even the dedicated stubborn ant
pays attention.

You were, in your life, more beautiful
than a flowering branch.
So I listened when you said,
"There is only one life and it is pain."
But I, who can hear the bee unlock

even the most tightly furled
onion blossom, no longer believe you.

Suitcase, Unaccompanied

Without consultation
the suitcase goes its own way
grateful for no destination.
It wasn't locked.
Took what it wanted.

Authorities require
for the purpose of detective work
a list of anything unusual
in the contents.
Ah, but how to tell?

The executioner's one red sock,
with hole. A child's tooth
in which sleeps an orphan,
grain of salt. Bound, maybe,
for the nameless cafe

where a woman
about to grow old
has her one good ear
still pressed gently against
the uncooked egg.

On the Outskirts of Town

Strictly off the record, officer,
here are the prints of my fingers,
each one an exitless maze:
four tropical fish, one dog, two cats,
deceased. And a marriage
so quickly over even a tornado
couldn't have tracked it
although not for lack of trying.

Take it all into custody.
Let it sleep guarded by the electronic eye
that sweeps but never shuts
on this clean metal cell.
What's kept out, less important
than what must stay. Even illness
couldn't flourish here, in the clear air
of such uncompromising observation.

Officer, I like the shine
of your tie tack: little handcuffs
that suggest anything
can be subdued; the glitter
of your badge, pure as holiday candy.
I'll ride with you every night,
an ordinary citizen
sick of looters, wife-beaters,

all the ways a life can go wrong
for lack of order. Now, when the snow falls
thin as the tears of a librarian working late,
let's drive the dark streets,
park for a smoke on the outskirts of town,
turn down the radio, watch
the moon appear through storm clouds
calm as the gravestone of a stranger.

The Thief of Light

He stole light and in his case, it was true—he couldn't help it. Snatched fire perched on church candles; lifted the golden highlights from his wife's eye. Secretly, the way any infidelity begins. He perfected his art on the lit tips of cigarettes, warning signals at railroad crossings. Still, the world only seemed to grow brighter. And his own heart, smaller, darker, shameful as a raisin. He culled electricity right out of the bedlamp bulb, chanted his lament on rosaries of coal. The King of the Thieves of Light! He will not be trifled with! Grows so thin that a new-moon night is enough to excite his hunger. And no one is trying to stop him. But even the old woman on the corner, the one who sits with her patient face turned toward this late winter sun can tell you. The world, in a way that is—as yet—unexplained, only grows brighter.

If I'd Been Born in Tennessee

I'd have long ago married somebody
named Sweet Pea Russell. Sour mash, shoot,
I guess. And my name'd be Rita Louise.
I'd find me a Chinaberry to sit up in
with old blind Henry's monkey and maybe
I'd play the banjo and maybe I'd just talk
monkey talk and wait for Sweet Pea to come looking.

There'd be no trouble telling how God's
got hold of the mockingbird's throat
making it tell its kinda repeat truth
just in a way you can't quite get hold of.
Or how the Lord's slinked his way
up the spine of the sunflower that leans over
eavesdropping on everything.

Reading aloud would be easier, too; vowels,
those old wheels going no place special
spinning their worn-outness on the red cart
those idiot twins drive around in,
their over-alls so dusty you ain't never
gonna tell what color they was to begin with.
There's rules. There's always rules.

But then there's what's got to be done.
And if I went out into the honeysuckle-
soaked night with someone I ain't naming.
And if we laid down on Double Wedding Ring
quilts and never slept the whole time and
never made much mind of if we got caught.
Well, I guess that's my own business.
I could give up

reading altogether and look for Jesus
in the garden with his gold scissors
cutting June-bugs and poke brush, black
snakes outta my way. I could say

God damn, just like that and be old,
the oldest woman ever was, without getting tired
of discoursing with whatever passes by—

three legged mongrel, hunter's moon,
or the reverend who wears the eye patch,
although the Lord ain't taken no sight
out of that eye. Holy past all telling, he talks
with no patience for the primrose path
which I do believe I have walked
all my life. Sour mash, shoot, I guess.

Taking Pleasure

In the almost empty cafe I light
a cigarette, taking pleasure
in blue hieroglyphics the smoke makes.
This is the first free time I've had
to myself in months. In Egypt
the beautiful, leathery flesh
of a mummy aches
for the sun's nonpartisan appraisal.
New arrival, at the next table,
an old man—in a voice clearly
meant to educate me—
tells his son how vulgar
cigarettes are, for nearly half an hour.
And so I pull the gun from my purse
and shoot him in the head. This
is not as violent as you might suppose.
He simply turns into a bush
of real roses. His son asks me
for a cigarette, smokes it calmly
then carries his father home
for transplanting, I assume.
My breakfast arrives: bacon, toast,
common cup of strong coffee,
one egg, yolk whole, sunny side up.

How Spring Appears This Time of Year in New England

In walks this lady, seventy five, maybe
eighty, wants the new look, something feisty.
Okay, so I roll her thin hair
then settle her under the dryer, old queen bee,
right out of a Saturday morning
monster movie.

She's a regular percussion section
rattling through movie magazines
like she's expecting some Latin type
named Rudolpho or Raoul to step out
of an illustration, sweep her off to a savannah,
scorch her with a lion-wild kiss.

I wasn't as careful as I should have been.
Her hair makes like lightning
in thin blue zig-zags, a real robot *do*.
She's got this smile would teach
a tornado patience. I try to give her
the messed up works for free but she pays

in full, washed cash, and you can see her
doing it. She'd soap each bill, pin
them all to a doll's laundry line, chirping
away the whole time—crazy old parakeet
so caught up in percolating her own song
seems to have forgot she's caught in the cage

for keeps. She counts out every coin to the last
shining dime, says, "Only three years old,
I'd steal blueberries, stuff myself fat
as a summer tick, just trying to turn some part
of myself blue. Now you've done it. And you
give it to me for a good price, too."

My Story as Told By Someone Else

Oh, little wren-brain, you believe yourself,
you really do, when you think
the trees have been talking to you.
Cut the human cerebellum in half—the pattern
of a tree reveals itself, scientifically
titled arbor vitae, you say, in ecstasy.

Leaf-blather, I think, a discovery
more trouble than it's worth. You insist,
self-appointed translator
of not just the arboreal choir but of cows
as well. Their udders at evening
swollen thick with the scent of honeysuckle.

Or so you say. Cows sway past while you,
mouth agape, kneel at the windowsill.
Little heart-of-a-kettle, as if you
had nothing better to do. As if praying.
You say they don't talk but rather shape
the silence into heliotheraphy:

gnat and radish, crow, cow
and cabbage butterfly. That the filament
in a bulb of glass passing into incandescence
is the same as a tulip's stamen, all light
and language intertwined in this.
Well, what kind of shape is that?

Air is air no matter what passes through.
Even your pine's just a photosynthesis machine.
At most, an unwilling host
to rooks who've cluttered it with nests
messy as sewing baskets. The great chain
of being's about eating. That's all. Teeth.

You, zoomorphic by degree, dabbling in botanomancy
have gone out of reach, climbed to the top

of a copper beech without stopping to check
what might inhabit the rest of the field.
Just now the mute bull lolls beneath you.
Maybe that will teach you.

Two Trout Fresh-Caught for Your Supper

Over the wire from America you said
you caught two trout
then threw them back for my return
so they'll live another month
until I put hook to line and cast
for them myself. You'll travel
to Florida. Life
is quiet and otherwise
fine. But how to translate
that? It's easier to have me gone?
Longing's not be wasted
over the crow-heavy wires? Or what?

So like me to take
the unspoken things for tangible
trouble ahead. So like you to tell,
abbreviated, what you think I want
to hear. Between us, an entire
ocean, a thousand shades
of indifferent blue.
So I took a walk down
the muddy path, mistrusting
love in every way I could, like throwing
money away or saying the wildflowers
were only terrible blade-bright lies.

Just then, when I had closed against
myself like a blindman's last
good eye, the wild peacock appeared
trailing its tail like the score
for an erotic opera over cow dung
and grass, its turquoise neck—
a perfect reproach against all doubt,
stark, in the cloud-heaped sky.
Then I walked back to find
the cook in the kitchen alone. "Look,"

she said, "in the pan, two trout
fresh-caught from Newbliss for your supper."

You might, might not, shrug
with nonchalance, call this
transatlantic coincidence.
But we'd both know better.
She'd cooked them the way
you do, in rich butter, little
salt, few herbs to keep
the flavor their own.
The flesh pink and sweet as all
we'd left unspoken—on each one
a gold slice of lemon, clear
as sun through cathedral glass.

Onion

No language is truly foreign.
Onion, for exmaple,
in Old French—

oignon or earlier, the Latin—
unio or *unionis,* translated
unity or pearl.

It is miraculous, somehow,
the girl in wedding dress,
and groom who can abandon

his hands to the unbuttoning
that two might exchange true gifts,
their bodies, earth

just earth, a little while animate.
Oh, onion, the tears you ask of us
contain no grief.

River

"The greatest cutting does not sever . . ."
                                    —Lao Tzu

Boulders long ago romanced by glaciers—
now a silky murmur of silt—inhabit me

peacefully, and only children, those who sleep
lightly, and the scarred understand.

What passes over, part of the cure:
clouds molded by a tranquil hand, heron-rise,

sunset. The depths are spangled
by a wily host: one trout leaps toward

light-proffered feast and just as fast sinks
back into a providence of clear current.

I am educated only in how things stay
whole but do not wholly stay.

Occasionally thunder booms a scrap
of old testament, but a sunrise

freely tosses solace, child's bouquet:
forget-me-not, pinks,

wood violet. Leave me, but I remain
with you and give you leave to be.

Carnegie Mellon Poetry

1981
A Little Faith, John Skoyles
Augers, Paula Rankin
Walking Home from the Icehouse, Vern Rutsala
Work and Love, Stephen Dunn
The Rote Walker, Mark Jarman
Morocco Journal, Richard Harteis
Songs of a Returning Soul, Elizabeth Libbey

1982
The Granary, Kim R. Stafford
Calling the Dead, C. G. Hanzlicek
Dreams Before Sleep, T. Alan Broughton
Sorting It Out, Anne S. Perlman
Love Is Not a Consolation; It Is a Light, Primus St. John

1983
The Going Under of the Evening Land, Mekeel McBride
Museum, Rita Dove
Air and Salt, Eve Shelnutt
Nightseasons, Peter Cooley

1984
Falling From Stardom, Jonathan Holden
Miracle Mile, Ed Ochester
Girlfriends and Wives, Robert Wallace
Earthly Purposes, Jay Meek
Not Dancing, Stephen Dunn
The Man in the Middle, Gregory Djanikian
A Heart Out of This World, David James
All You Have in Common, Dara Wier

1985
Smoke From the Fires, Michael Dennis Browne
Full of Lust and Good Usage, Stephen Dunn (2nd edition)
Far and Away, Mark Jarman
Anniversary of the Air, Michael Waters
To the House Ghost, Paula Rankin
Midwinter Transport, Anne Bromley

1987
Some Gangster Pain, Gillian Conoley
Other Children, Lawrence Raab
Internal Geography, Richard Harteis
The Van Gogh Notebook, Peter Cooley
A Circus of Needs, Stephen Dunn (2nd edition)
Ruined Cities, Vern Rutsala
Places and Stories, Kim R. Stafford

1988
Preparing to Be Happy, T. Alan Broughton
Red Letter Days, Mekeel McBride
The Abandoned Country, Thomas Rabbitt